SPEED! BOATS

Jenifer Corr Morse

BLACKBIRCH PRESS, INC.

WOODBRIDGE, CONNECTICUT

To Stephen Langdon Morse—
Someday soon.
–JCM

Printed in Belgium

10 9 8 7 6 5 4 3 2

Photo Credits
Cover (center), pages 1, 4: Stena Line; cover (top), pages 22-23: courtesy of Lockheed Martin; cover (bottom right), pages 8-9: Paragon Mann Ltd; cover (bottom left), page 10: ©Andrew Woodley/PPL; page 13: ©Nigel Rolstone; Cordaiy Photo Library Ltd/CORBIS; pages 6-7: Naval Historical Foundation; pages 14-15: Hoverspeed Limited; pages 16-17: Ian Shiffman; page 18: ©Hulton Getty/Archive Photos; page 20: ©U.S. Navy Photo, courtesy Woods Hole Oceanographic Institution;.

Library of Congress Cataloging-in-Publication Data
Morse, Jenifer Corr.
        Boats / by Jenifer Morse.
        p. cm. — (Speed!)
Includes index.
        ISBN 1-56711-468-7 (hardcover)
        1. Jet boats—Juvenile literature. 2. Boats and boating—Juvenile literature. 3. Ships—Juvenile literature. [1. Jet boats. 2. Motorboats. 3. Boats and boating. 4. Submarines (Ships)] I. Title. II. Speed! (Woodbridge, Conn.)

VM348.5 .M67 2001
623.8—dc21   00-011917

Contents

The HSS 1500 is almost the
same size as a football field.

Stena HSS 1500
The world's largest fast ferry

The Stena HSS 1500 is truly an amazing vehicle. It is the world's largest fast ferry, measuring 406 feet (124 m) long and 131 feet (40 m) wide. That's almost the same size as a football field! It can carry 1,500 passengers and 375 cars. In fact, the HSS 1500 is able to load 1,500 tons, which is 5 times more cargo than any other ferry!

Despite its great size, the HSS—which stands for high-speed sea service—is also a speedy boat. It can travel at about 40 knots, or 46 miles (74 km) per hour. It's even able to cruise through 13-foot- (4-m) high waves at that speed without disturbing its passengers.

●≡Fast ≡Fact ●

The HSS 1500 uses 4 gas turbine engines that produce 100,000 horsepower. That's equal to the horsepower produced by a jumbo jet! These powerful engines are split between the catamaran's two hulls.

The HSS 1500 operates using the latest technology. The bridge of the ship looks very much like the cockpit of an airplane. Inside, a very sophisticated electronics system controls the vessel. It even has a built-in satellite docking system.

Passengers have plenty of room to move around on this giant ship. Most activities and services are located around the 43,055-square-foot (4,000-sq-m) deck. Besides enjoying the spectacular view, travelers can shop, watch videos, play interactive computer games, or just relax in the lounge. Children can keep busy in the activity center. There's even a McDonald's on board for hungry travelers!

Trieste

The only submersible to reach the deepest part of the ocean

The *Trieste*—operated by Swiss scientist Jacques Piccard and U.S. Navy Lieutenant Don Walsh—reached an amazing depth of 35,800 feet (10,912 m) on January 23, 1960. This historic dive occurred in the Challenger Deep, located in the Mariana Trench. This area of the Pacific Ocean is the lowest known point in the world. It is so deep that if Mount Everest were dropped to this depth, its highest peak would still be a mile below the surface of the water!

The 50-foot- (15-m) long *Trieste* is a type of boat called a bathyscaphe. The outer vessel was filled with gasoline and contains a smaller, steel sphere that is attached to the base of the boat. To make the ship dive down, gasoline is released and replaced by seawater. Because seawater is heavier than gasoline, the vessel slowly sinks as more water is brought into

The Trieste *descended almost 7 miles (11 km) below the surface of the Pacific.*

The Trieste *is lowered into the water.*

the vessel. There is also 9 tons of steel on the bottom of the craft to help it sink. The crew sat in the 6-foot- (1.8-m) diameter sphere. They could see out of a small glass window that measured 8 inches (20 cm) thick.

Once Piccard and Walsh reached the ocean floor, they were surprised to see fish at that great depth. The water pressure at that spot—almost 7 miles (11 km) below the surface—was more than 100,000 tons. That's about 1,000 times more than the pressure at sea level! When they were ready to return to the surface, the crew slowly released the steel from the bottom of the boat.

=Fast =Fact

After setting the record for the world's deepest dive, the *Trieste* was later used to collect information on several shipwrecks. It is now on display at the Navy Museum in Washington D.C.

VSV Wave Piercer

This craft can cruise above and below the water.

The *VSV Wave Piercer* can do things that few boats can. While racing along the surface of the water at a top speed of 57 miles (91.7 km) per hour, the boat can tear through waves without losing momentum. It can even speed below the water's surface without slowing down or endangering its crew, who sit in an enclosed cockpit. In fact, if the ship is knocked upside down by a wave, it will automatically turn right side up again!

The *Wave Piercer* is 53 feet (16 m) long. It has a 9-foot (2.7-m) beam and can float in as little as 3 feet (1 m) of water. It has 2 engines that each produce 660 horsepower. The fuel tank holds 660 gallons

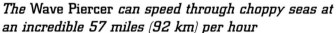

The Wave Piercer *can speed through choppy seas at an incredible 57 miles (92 km) per hour*

(2,489 l) of gasoline, and the ship can travel 500 miles (805 km) before refueling.

Because of its underwater abilities and camouflaged coloring, this special boat is often used by the military. The sparkly white hull

⬤ ⋮Fast ⋮Fact ⬤

One reason this boat can zip through rough water is its streamlined shape. The front of the *Wave Piercer* is long and pointy, kind of like a swordfish. This shape helps prevent the boat from being pushed backward by the force of the waves.

looks like the crest of a wave on the water. On board, the two-person crew can monitor the ship's progress with its advanced equipment. A depth sounder, speedometer, radar screen, and computerized maps show the crew what's going on around them.

Yellow Pages Endeavour
The world's fastest sailing vessel

On October 26, 1993, the *Yellow Pages Endeavour* cruised into the record books as the world's fastest sailing vessel. The ship, piloted by Simon McKeon and Tim Daddo, averaged a top speed of 53.5 miles (86.1 km) per hour. To get a qualifying top speed, the ship had to make two runs over the 1,640-foot- (500-m) long course at Sandy Point near Melbourne, Australia, within a certain time. The final time was an average of the two runs.

The *Endeavour* had to make the runs many times before it qualified for the world record in the allotted time. Unlike most boats, the *Endeavour* has one stiff, 39-foot- (11.8-m) high sail

Fast Fact

The two-person crew rides in the cockpit that is suspended on a long pole. It is located opposite the large sail, and the crew has to balance very carefully to keep the *Endeavour* from tipping over.

that is permanently anchored to the boat and can't swing in different directions. This makes the boat very fast, but it can only sail in one direction. Because the boat could not turn around by itself to make the second run, it had to be towed. This took some time and often disqualified the speedy ship.

The *Yellow Pages Endeavour* is 35 feet (10.6 m) long. It is known as a trifoiler because it has three short planing hulls, or hydrofoils, which balance the boat above the water. Instead of banging up against the waves with a broad hull, the hydrofoils on the *Endeavour* glide over the top of the sea.

The Yellow Pages Endeavour *can sail at a top speed of more than 53 miles (86 km) per hour.*

SeaCat Ferry

The world's fastest passenger ferry

Cruising at a top speed of 48 miles (77.2 km) per hour, the SeaCat is the fastest passenger ferry in the world. SeaCats are powered by 4 diesel engines capable of producing more than 4,800 horsepower. The engines rotate 750 times each minute, pulling water in and driving it back out. This process lifts the large boat's hulls up above the water and the waves, allowing it to maintain a quick pace.

One SeaCat ferry sails in the English Channel, carrying travelers between England and France. During a trip, it can carry up to 600 passengers and 80 cars. This ferry, which is classified as a catamaran, has two light-weight aluminum hulls. It is 241 feet (73.4 m) long, with a beam measuring 86 feet (26.2 m). The SeaCat weighs a total of 3,003 tons, and can sail in as little as 8 feet (2.4 m) of water when it is fully loaded.

SeaCat ferries also operate in the Irish Sea and the Scottish Isles. The SeaCat ferry *Hoverspeed Great Britain* holds some impressive records. It was the first vehicle-carrying catamaran when it debuted in 1990. Also, during its first voyage between New York and Cornwall, it became the fastest ship ever to cross the Atlantic Ocean.

The four engines of a SeaCat help to lift the boat above the waves as it speeds through the water.

● **Fast Fact** ●

It's not surprising that the same engineers that helped create the Ferrari—one of the fastest cars in the world—also designed the SeaCat.

Princess Anne

Crossed the English Channel in the fastest time

The *Princess Anne* was one of two SNR4 Mark III hovercraft used to ferry both passengers and cars across the English Channel. On September 14, 1995, the *Princess Anne* completed the 23-mile- (37-km) long journey in just 22 minutes. It normally takes a hovercraft 35 minutes to sail between Calais, France, and Dover, England. This hovercraft remained the fastest ferry service across the Channel until it was retired and replaced by SeaCat ferries in October 2000.

The *Princess Anne* and her sister ship, the *Princess Margaret,* debuted in the late 1960s. Each hovercraft ran on four 3,800-horsepower Rolls Royce gas turbine engines. Together these engines could produce

Powerful fans lift the hovercraft above the water.

The Princess Anne *could reach a top speed of 75 miles (121 km) an hour.*

48,060 pounds (21,800 kg) of thrust! The hovercraft were designed to travel up to 75 miles (121 km) per hour, but the speed limit in the English Channel restricted them to under 55 miles (93 km) an hour.

A hovercraft can float over both water and land by traveling on a cushion of air. The *Princess Anne* has a flexible rubber skirt surrounding the bottom of the boat. When inflated by 4 powerful lift fans and propellers, the skirt raises the craft up 10 feet (3 m) into the air! Most of the air stays trapped under the skirt, allowing the vessel to float.

> **≡Fast ≡Fact**
>
> The *Princess Anne* was also the world's largest commercial hovercraft. It measures184 feet (56.3 m) long and weighs 335 tons. It was capable of carrying up to 418 passengers, 16 crew, and 60 cars.

SS United States

Fastest ocean liner to cross the Atlantic Ocean

The SS United States *sailed at an average speed of 40 miles (64 km) per hour.*

On her maiden voyage from New York to Le Havre, France, the *SS United States* completed the trip in only 3 days, 10 hours, and 40 minutes. The *SS United States* made the 3,391-mile (5,457-km) journey at an average speed of about 41 miles (66 km) per hour. She became the fastest ocean liner to cross the Atlantic Ocean and was awarded the Blue Riband Award for her accomplishment.

What is most impressive about the short crossing time is that the *SS United States* did not even sail at full speed. The ship was equipped to generate 240,000 horsepower, but it did not exceed 158,000 horsepower for the voyage!

The *SS United States* is 990 feet (302 m) long— approximately the length of 5 city blocks. It is 12 stories high and 101 feet (31 m) wide. This massive ship could

> ## ●≡*Fast* ≡*Fact* ●
>
> The ***SS United States*** **was one of the most impressive vessels ever created in America. The giant ocean liner was built in Virginia at a cost of $70 million, and first set sail in 1952.**

carry 10,306 tons of fuel and cruise nonstop at a speed of 40 miles (64 km) an hour for 11,510 miles (18,523 km). The *SS United States* also had 4 propellers that each measured 18 feet (5.5 m) in diameter.

This speedy ocean liner could carry 1,972 passengers and 1,066 crew. The ship's chefs prepared about 9,000 meals each day, plus afternoon tea and midnight snacks. The ship was also the first of its size to be completely air-conditioned. In fact, it could easily cool a theater three times the size of Radio Music Hall in New York City!

*The **SS United States** was roughly the same length as five city blocks.*

Spirit of Australia

The fastest boat in the world

Ken Warby sailed the Spirit of Australia at a record 317 miles (511 km) per hour.

The *Spirit of Australia* is the fastest boat in the world and has held its record for more than 20 years. To compete for the world water speed title, a boat must make two back-to-back trips across a course and take the average speed of the two runs.

Ken Warby, an Australia native, actually designed and built the *Spirit of Australia* in his backyard. He fitted it with a Westinghouse jet engine capable of producing 6,000 horsepower. He first won the world water speed record

with the boat in 1977, reaching a top average speed of 288 miles (463 km) per hour. Then, one year later, he shattered his old record when he achieved a top average speed of 317.6 miles (511.1 km) an hour. That's almost five times the speed limit on most state highways! Both record attempts were completed on the Blowering Dam in Australia.

Racing hydroplane boats is a very dangerous sport. As the boat increases its speed, it is difficult to keep it in the water. The front of the boat can easily pull up and take off like an airplane. When this happens at around 300 miles (482 km) per hour, the pressure on the vehicle equals around 3,500 pounds (1,588 kg) per square inch. This causes the boat to break into many tiny pieces, killing the driver.

Sea Cliff

A manned submarine that can dive down 20,000 feet (6,100 m)

The *Sea Cliff* is a manned, non-fighter submarine. It was first launched in 1968, and went into service for the U.S. Navy in 1970. The submarine was originally built to reach depths of 6,500 feet (1,981 m), but was upgraded in the early 1980s to go much deeper. In March 1985, the *Sea Cliff* reached the depth of 20,000 feet (6,100 m) during a dive off the Pacific coast of Central America.

The Sea Cliff can travel 2.5 miles (4 km) an hour as it operates 20,000 feet (6,100 m) below the ocean's surface.

The Navy used the *Sea Cliff* mainly for military research. It could also locate and recover planes, boats, and equipment that had sunk. To help guide it, the submarine had short-range sonar and external lights. The craft used its two movable arms to examine and handle objects. It was also able to take pictures with both video and still cameras.

The *Sea Cliff* is 26 feet (7.9 m) long. The 3-person crew sits in a 7-foot- (2- m) diameter metal sphere that is surrounded by a fiber-glass hull. Traveling at 1 mile (1.6 km) per hour, the sub can remain underwater for 8 hours. If the craft increases its speed to 2.5 miles (4 km) per hour, it is only able to stay submerged for about an hour.

In 1998 the Navy decided to take the *Sea Cliff* out of service because of budget cutbacks. The vessel is currently at Woods Hole Oceanographic Institute in Massachusetts. Even though the sub was designed for military purposes, it could be adapted for scientific research. Because of its deep-diving abilities, it would give scientists access to 98 percent of the world's ocean floor.

Fast Fact

In addition to the *Sea Cliff,* there are only 3 other submersibles in service today that can reach depths of 20,000 feet (6,100 m).

Sea Shadow

One of the most advanced military boats in the world

Until recently, the U.S. Navy's *Sea Shadow* has been kept top secret. In fact, it was even put together inside a giant barge so that nobody would be able to see how the ship was assembled, or that it even existed! The *Sea Shadow* was also only tested at night so nobody could take a good look at it.

Some of the Navy's most advanced technology is used aboard the **Sea Shadow.**

The most unusual thing about the *Sea Shadow* is its design. With its odd-shaped angles, it resembles a floating pyramid. These angles help to keep enemy radar from picking up the ship as it sails by.

The *Sea Shadow* program began in the mid-1980s, and was first introduced to the public in 1993. The main purpose of the ship is to test out design features for use in future Navy vessels. One design goal is to reduce the crew size of a ship. Many of the *Sea Shadow's* features have been automated, which means its crew can be limited to only 10 members.

After suspending testing for five years, the *Sea Shadow* resumed testing in the San Francisco Bay in 1999. It mainly simulated attacks on other Navy ships to see how they would respond during an emergency. The Navy is currently testing various other advanced technology that would improve the capability of this stealthy, super fighting machine.

Fast Fact

The *Sea Shadow* is 168 feet (49.9 m) long and has a 68-foot- (20.7-m) long beam. It has a steel hull and superstructure, and weighs 64 tons.

Glossary

bathyscaphe: an undersea vehicle that is used for deep-sea exploration
bridge: a platform over the deck of a ship
catamaran: a boat that has two hulls that are joined together
horsepower: a unit for measuring the power of an engine
hull: the frame or body of a boat or ship
sonar: an instrument that is used to calculate how deep the water is or where underwater objects are. It works by sending sound waves through the water and listening for when they bounce back off something

For More Information

Books

Bornhoft, Simon. *High-Speed Boats* (The Need For Speed). Minneapolis, MN: Lerner Publications, 1999.
Graham, Ian. *Boats* (Built For Speed). Chatham, NJ: Raintree Steck-Vaughn, 1999.
Green, Michael. *Submarines* (Land and Sea). Mankato, MN: Capstone Press, 1998.

Web Site

Woods Hole Oceanographic Institute
See photos of and learn more about ships and underwater vehicles—
www.marine.whoi.edu.

Index

623.8
MOR   Morse, Jenifer Corr
        Boats

DATE DUE

623.8
MOR   Morse, Jenifer Corr
        Boats

DATE DUE	BORROWER'S NAME	ROOM NUMBER

DEMCO